LOG ⏻N
and LEARN

LOG ON and LEARN

how to QUICKLY *and* EASILY CREATE ONLINE COURSES *that*

EXPAND YOUR BRAND, CULTIVATE CUSTOMERS,

and MAKE YOU MONEY WHILE YOU SLEEP

ADAM WITTY

Published by Advantage, Charleston, South Carolina.
Member of Advantage Media Group.

ADVANTAGE is a registered trademark and the Advantage colophon is a trademark of Advantage Media Group, Inc.

Printed in the United States of America.

ISBN: 978-159932-410-4
LCCN: 2013936056

This publication is designed to provide accurate and authoritative information in regard to the subject matter covered. It is sold with the understanding that the publisher is not engaged in rendering legal, accounting, or other professional services. If legal advice or other expert assistance is required, the services of a competent professional person should be sought.

Advantage Media Group is proud to be a part of the Tree Neutral® program. Tree Neutral offsets the number of trees consumed in the production and printing of this book by taking proactive steps such as planting trees in direct proportion to the number of trees used to print books. To learn more about Tree Neutral, please visit **www.treeneutral.com**. To learn more about Advantage's commitment to being a responsible steward of the environment, please visit **www.advantagefamily.com/green**

Advantage Media Group is a publisher of business, self-improvement, and professional development books and online learning. We help entrepreneurs, business leaders, and professionals share their Stories, Passion, and Knowledge to help others Learn & Grow. Do you have a manuscript or book idea that you would like us to consider for publishing? Please visit **advantagefamily.com** or call **1.866.775.1696**.

This book is dedicated to the entrepreneurs, business leaders, and professionals who have Stories, Passion, and Knowledge to share with the world.

TABLE OF CONTENTS

....

SECTION THREE
THE THREE STEPS TO CREATING YOUR ONLINE LEARNING

....

REGISTER
YOUR BOOK

AND ACCESS FREE RESOURCES !

It doesn't matter where you are in the world, Adam can help you share your Stories, Passion, and Knowledge with the world in the form of online learning courses.

Visit LOGONANDLEARNBOOK.COM to access these free resources:

 **RECEIVE** a subscription to the Author Success University™ monthly teleseminars wherein successful authors and book marketing experts reveal their tips and tricks for marketing and growing a business.

 **REGISTER** for a webinar led by Adam Witty: "How to Quickly and Easily Create Online Courses that Expand Your Brand, Cultivate Customers, and Make You Money While You Sleep."

 **COMPLETE** Advantage's Online Learning Questionnaire and receive a complimentary Discovery Call with an acquisitions editor to help you determine if your book, keynote speech, or content are worth turning into an online course.

 **REQUEST** an Info-Pak and live demonstration to discover how transforming your content into online learning can help you and your business best.

ACCESS ALL OF THE ABOVE FREE RESOURCES BY REGISTERING YOUR BOOK AT
LOGONANDLEARNBOOK.COM

SECTION ONE

the

BIG IDEA

CHAPTER 1

THE TIMES THEY ARE A-CHANGIN'

Why Online Learning Matters

L ook around you. Right now. Yes, I'm talking to you. Count how many technological devices you see nearby. Is there a phone? A computer? How about a tablet?

Odds are, whether you're sipping a caffeine-rich beverage in a cozy coffee shop, catching up on the morning's news while riding the subway, or peering out of an airplane window to a world thousands of feet below, you are surrounded by technology in action. All around you, your fellow peers are tapping into a vibrant, dazzling world in order to do a variety of things: conduct business, e-mail photos, pay bills, shop, or double-check directions. We live in a wired world that contains over 2.1 billion Internet connections and 5.3 billion mobile subscriptions.

E-commerce, search engines, e-mail agents, shopping sites, and social networking platforms are the predominant online forums for interaction. However, a new frontier is emerging, one that will transform how businesses, schools, and universities operate. This platform revolutionizes the way that content is delivered, making the ability to reach new audiences virtually limitless.

This platform is online learning.

So, what does *online learning* really mean? How will it help you build your business? How will it help you expand your audience? How will it help you have more impact? How do you plug in to online learning? *(Pun intended.)*

Well, let's consider the experience of a man named Webster. Webster is a professional very much like you. Okay, maybe he's a little shorter. Webster loves his career—he helps people learn and grow. Webster is a professional speaker and consultant. He makes great money (well over six figures a year). He's always the designated cameraman at his kids' performances, and every week he treats his wife to dinner at their favorite sushi restaurant. Webster has built his reputation up in order to be asked to speak at events with thousands of attendees. He stays fit by jogging in 5K races for charity and acting as first baseman on the local recreational baseball team.

Here's the riddle: Webster has the exact same job as you do. How does Webster possibly have the time or energy to lead a balanced lifestyle, spending time with his family and community, while doing the same work you do?

It's impossible, you say. Yet, actually, it's more than possible.

I'm here to share Webster's secret with you. Before he turned to online learning, he also juggled the hectic travel schedule that you manage now, going to a new city almost every week, booking speaking events in faraway places, and playing phone tag with clients, all the while struggling to find the energy to write his book or create new content during late nights, when he was exhausted. Webster often had to cancel the time he needed to work on his own business when clients booked him. He never felt he was reaching as many people as he could. He felt he could make more money and have more impact if he just had more time.

At that point, Webster loved his work, but logistics prevented him from increasing his audience and living a balanced lifestyle. Webster was working hard, no doubt about it, but Webster was unsure whether he was working in a smart way.

Does that sound familiar?

To solve this problem, Webster turned to online learning, expanding his audience and his message without ever having to book another hotel room night or make another connecting flight. Here are a few of the steps he took:

- Webster worked with a professional course designer to create a blueprint of a series of online courses he could shoot at his hometown video studio.

- Webster developed and launched an online university with courses based on the content in his speeches, workshops, and training.

- Webster engaged the support of a professional publisher to build, distribute, market, and sell his online courses worldwide.

- Webster began to cross-promote his online courses to existing speaking and consulting clients; doing so provided them more value, through a proven mechanism, and reinforced his key speaking and consulting curriculum.

- Webster saw growth in his business and gained more time in his schedule for what he really wanted to focus on: his next project and time to travel—for fun—with his family.

Today, students from all over the world login to Webster's site at whatever hours are convenient for them, and they study his courses, which are filled with video lectures, interactive quizzes, and hands-on exercises. After completing the coursework, they take a final test for certification. Employers and business partners contact Webster for virtual workshops after hearing referrals from his clients. His books, often required reading material for these courses, are selling like never before. Webster is reaching more eyes and ears than ever before, and he's never had so much flexible time in which to do what he wants to do.

If Webster's plan sounds good to you, his story could be yours. (Yes, I did choose the name *Webster* to reflect the role that the Web plays in this new approach to work.) By migrating your valuable content and expertise to an online format, namely online courses, you'll have more time, reach a wider audience, cut down on your travel, and earn more income than ever before.

Online education is a powerful method you can use to take your business to the next level and reach the mass audience of online learners waiting to hear from you.

To give you a sense of the level of interest in and adoption of online learning today, consider the following:

- Over 50 percent of brick-and-mortar colleges offer online learning as an option for students. Today many colleges offer entire online programs and degrees in various fields, including business administration, computer science, forensics, information technology, health services, nursing, and more.

- Students benefit from online courses, since they use less fuel driving to and from a campus. Students can work a day job while taking courses in the evenings or on lunch breaks. When taking online courses, those students located in remote areas can access material that they otherwise could not retrieve. Each student in an online course can learn at his or her own pace.

- For universities, the advantages of online learning are vast. Classrooms are freed up for other courses. Professors can spend more time on research, projects, grading, and student support. While at one point a class could only contain 30 students for an entire five-month semester, now over 1,000 students can enroll in the same course. Enrollment has skyrocketed, resulting in more education for more people, and of course more tuition for universities, too.

- In the business world, 61 percent of professional associations employ some form of online learning, from webinars to self-paced courses. Beyond that, 25 percent of associations plan to begin using online learning in the next year. Every year this number grows because more associations recognize online learning's importance. Online learning is the future of professional development.

- Overall, businesses and universities cite the primary reasons for adopting online learning as being more cost effective and more convenient for employees and students, as well as being more capable of supporting higher numbers of learners.

- Leaders of private businesses are flocking to online learning to meet their employees' professional development needs. With travel costs on the rise, and out-of-office lost productivity a continuous concern, companies are providing ongoing continuing education to their employees from the comfort and convenience of those employees' computers.

Perhaps one of the most resounding endorsements and prophetic statements for online education and its growth is by well-known business leader John Chambers, CEO of Cisco Systems. "The next big **killer application** on the Internet is going to be education. **Education over the Internet is going to be so big** it is going to make e-mail usage look like a rounding error," says Chambers.

If you're excited by and curious about the prospect of how you and your business can ride this emerging tidal wave, read on. This book is for content leaders, gurus, and professional speakers who have information to share. In the next chapter, you'll learn about the practical benefits of online education and the steps to building a profitable business in online learning.

CHAPTER 2

THE BIG PICTURE

How You Fit In

Where do we begin? With what you already have, of course. Whether you have a keynote speech, a book or books, CDs, DVDs, speaking engagements, or other proprietary content, all of these materials form the foundation of your online content. After all, we're just migrating your content to an online format—not reinventing all of your hard work.

Online education provides one more, much bigger way for customers to access your knowledge and connect with you and each other.

By providing them with online learning, you give customers more ways to connect with you, more ways to give money to you, and more ways to learn from you. This online network of relationships you will create with your customers is often called a *community*. With the proper setup, this community will grow and strengthen on its own, needing little of your time or energy on an ongoing basis.

Ask yourself what goals you have to take your business to the next level. What's your big-picture idea?

If it's wider reach, online education opens you up to the teeming world of international learners seeking to educate themselves. Today, more than ever before, hundreds of thousands of students and working professionals prefer to learn online for the sake of convenience.

If it's a closer connection to students, the passion and expertise you bring can be reflected in well-designed online courses just as much as it could be presented if you were standing in front of them teaching and speaking. Multimedia elements such as video, audio, and more will convey your voice and appearance to them, establishing a connection that reaches beyond books and paper.

If it's increased profit margins and maximizing investment returns, consider what it would mean to make money while you sleep. We'll talk more about this concept in future chapters, but what it means, essentially, is that your online classes do your work for you at all hours of the day. Customers (or "students") register and purchase your courses (or "pay tuition") online through your site as you go about your daily business. Additionally, the costs of hosting an online university are minor in comparison to the varying overhead costs of travel, hotel stays, purchasing and printing materials, creating CDs and DVDs, and so forth.

If it's rescuing hours and adding them back into your day, consider the differences between offering constant, continually available online courses that operate automatically and having to spend your time scheduling consulting and coaching sessions and booking speaking engagements throughout the year. You're no longer at the mercy of your clients' or meeting planners' schedules. Sure, you can still travel, but only for the engagements you truly want or need to be at in person.

In short, online education is here to stay, and tapping into its vast power is the key to achieving your big-picture goals. You'll reap the benefits of increased income, time, energy, and audience by developing an online university for your customers.

the

TOP FIVE

• *reasons*

to turn your BOOK, KEYNOTE SPEECH, *or* CONTENT *into an* ONLINE COURSE

In this section, you will learn the top five reasons for turning your content into an online course. As you read, consider the application questions at the end of each chapter in relation to how each reason could be an advantage to your business. You may be surprised at the potential your content has for becoming a flourishing and popular online course.

CHAPTER 3

···

MAKE MONEY WHILE YOU SLEEP

You have probably heard of George Burns, the famous comedian. George once said, "Don't stay in bed unless you can make money in bed." Little did George know that millions of business professionals would live according to his advice. Millions of professionals are making money as they sleep: songwriters and authors who earn royalties, insurance agents who earn residuals, and stockholders who earn interest on their holdings. It's like magic money—you open your mailbox, and there's a check, the money available for you to spend or save. How did this happen? Well, you've let your initial hard work do the residual work for you long after you completed it.

Many professionals, however, still trade hours for dollars. They work, and then they get paid. They work, and then they get paid. The process repeats itself. If you are a consultant, you get paid for the time you provide to your client. If you are a speaker, you get paid when you make an in-person appearance. If you are a doctor, you get paid when you see a patient. If you are an accountant, you get paid when you complete a client's tax return. If you are an attorney, you get paid by the hour. Remember, attorneys invented the phrase *billable hours.*

Online learning can grow your passive income dramatically. Imagine having the ability to create a product once, launch it online, and never have to execute another measure to drive continuous, recurring revenue, month after month. In developing an online course, you set up a steady stream of income that will build year after year.

Imagine what it would be like if you didn't have to speak live, and you still got paid.

Imagine what it would be like if you didn't have to trade hours for dollars.

Imagine what it would be like if you didn't have to get on an airplane and travel to get paid.

Imagine what it would be like if you could bring your content and expertise right into the customer or client's home or office.

If you're still thinking this idea sounds too good to be true, consider the words of Jack Messman, former CEO of computer networking giant Novell. "Online learning will rapidly become one of the most **cost-effective** ways to educate the world's expanding workforce," says Messman.

As a professional speaker or consultant, you might be stuck in the rut I just mentioned, trading hours for dollars or having to travel to make speaking or consulting engagements prior to getting paid.

Online learning is the first significant advancement for speakers, consultants, and content leaders in years. The reason is that today, more than any other time in history, people are more comfortable doing things online than in-person. Today, a majority of Americans would rather purchase a book on Amazon.com than walk into a Barnes & Noble bookstore. Today, a majority of Americans prefer to watch a movie on Netflix instead of driving to the movie theater. Today, many Americans would rather look for a perfect mate online via Match.com instead of meeting strangers at a bar.

For the same reasons that people prefer to make key purchases online rather than in person, many students and business professionals are opting to continue their education online rather than in person. Traditional brick-and-mortar college enrollments are moving down as online enrollments are skyrocketing. Attendance at seminars, conferences, and trade shows is limping along, showing no noticeable signs of growth. In contrast, professional development online learning outfits like Lynda.com are exploding, adding thousands of new students every day.

Online learning is convenient and cost effective for the student and the person or company paying the tuition. For the instructor (you), online learning is more convenient and cost effective as well. Lower overhead costs and higher profits are all but guaranteed with online learning. It's a win-win for you and your learners.

Application Questions: Think about your own time spent traveling, speaking, and connecting with clients: Could you benefit by making money while you sleep? Could you benefit by rescuing some hours and adding them back into your day? What would you do with that extra time?

CHAPTER 4

CREATE A HIGHER-VALUE DELIVERABLE FOR YOUR CUSTOMERS

Much of my career has been in the book-publishing business. In fact, my company, Advantage Media Group, is a leading publisher of business, self-improvement, and professional development books and online content. After working with hundreds of authors, and overseeing hundreds of new titles published every year, I've spent more than my fair share of time around books. The truth is, I love books.

That is, except for one big, glaring problem.

Each author spends hundreds of hours laboring over his or her masterpiece. The author takes all of the knowledge he or she has accumulated in a lifetime on a particular topic, pours it into two hundred pages, and sells it for $20.

Everything that the author knows then becomes available for just $20. How is that for a smack in the face? With e-books forcing prices down even further, there is a tremendous race to the bottom by publishers and authors in offering lower and lower prices for books. It is very difficult for authors to make much money through book sales. That is why you must create higher-value products for your customers.

Perhaps you already have explored other ways of creating more value for customers: converting your audio into CDs or mp3s, which you can make available for download; filming your speeches or segments of your presentation for DVDs or streaming online video; or developing workbooks and action guides that refer back to your original book.

Multiple modalities, or channels for learning, equal a greater value for customers. This statement is supported by the well-known fact that everyone learns in a different way. Auditory learners absorb knowledge most efficiently through hearing the lessons; visual learners retain material optimally by reading or processing images; and kinetic learners can demonstrate their newfound understanding best after physically performing exercises or tasks designed to reinforce messages or learning concepts.

By providing your learners with multiple modalities, such as online audio, video, testing, and more, you present a higher-value deliverable. You give them more ways to absorb your content. Today's learners are swept up in a fast-paced world of distractions and messages; by offering them online learning, you offer a higher-value deliverable that is guaranteed to increase the knowledge transfer from you to the learners over books or tapes.

Application Questions: What modalities do you currently offer your audience? What new channels would be a good fit for your material and audience? If your audience is mobile, consider offering courses that are accessible by mobile devices. Your online university can provide many channels of accessibility.

CHAPTER 5

BUILD BETTER CUSTOMERS

G rowing up in Florida, I became a Jimmy Buffett fan. With sea legs and thin blood, I routinely caught myself whistling, "Cheeseburger in Paradise."

Now, when it comes to being a fan of Jimmy Buffett, or any artist for that matter, you know that such fans come in many forms and varieties. To start, you have typical fans: people who buy Jimmy Buffett songs on the iTunes store and immediately stop the radio dial when they hear a Buffett song. Then, of course, you have the next level of fans. These are the folks who have seen Buffett live in concert. These might also be the folks who go out of their way to find his Margaritaville restaurant when visiting Key West. At the top of the fan pyramid, Jimmy Buffett has his "true fans."

You might be wondering what a "true fan" is. In the Buffett world, these individuals are affectionately referred to as "Parrotheads." True fans drive for hours in sleet and snow to see Buffett perform live. True fans purchase Buffett's tri-ple-platinum, collector's edition CD set that's priced at $400. True fans have read Jimmy Buffett's book and purchased a copy for each family member's birthday.

As a speaker, author, and guru, you are an artist, no different from Jimmy Buffett. Your job is to take casual fans and turn them into true fans.

How would you describe your typical client or customer? Your client base may include many of the following: business owners, sales professionals, middle managers, tech-savvy individuals, tech-challenged folks, men, women, young people, middle-aged persons, and advanced-age individuals.

You have probably already spent time getting to know your audience members in order to reach them and under-stand them. Is your typical customer the same as your ideal customer?

As entrepreneurs, we are all in the business of customer development. You want to attract customers who will appre-ciate your work and apply it to their own lives in meaningful ways. My client and friend Dan Kenney is quick to point out that all entrepreneurs and business owners should think of themselves as ranchers. Dan says that the object of business is to go out, get a herd of customers, and then build a fence around that herd, so they don't go off and start grazing in other pastures. Of course, you have to feed your herd continually so it grows and provides you with more milk, or, to extend the comparison, profits.

So, how do you build up this customer base, one that is more in tune with these goals and philosophies? Consumption is key, as is compliance. Building better customers means getting them to eat from your trough continuously, which in turn creates a following of people who have truly bought in to your beliefs, theories, and practices. They are loyal, and with their loyalty they give you compliance. Their compliance helps them to retain the information contained within your courses, apply it to their lives and businesses, and ultimately share it with colleagues and other connections. They get more out of what you teach. Having this base of advocates, or true fans for your work, will increase your range of impact exponentially.

As an entrepreneur, you must always be asking "What is next?". Anticipate the customers' needs before they themselves comprehend those needs. The customers who are currently eating at your trough will eventually tire of the meal you are serving. Unless you differentiate and come up with something new, they will leave. Learning, by nature, never ends. Course 101 leads to course 102, which leads to course 201, leading to course 202. With online learning, you can create a product that will provide plentiful consumption opportunities for customers. Just as each time you dine at a restaurant you become more loyal to that restaurant, the same is true with continuous consumption of your content online; this consumption creates a more compliant (and loyal) customer.

Application Questions: When you build better customers, you'll be rewarded with more loyal customers, higher referrals, and overall increased effectiveness. Referrals from one customer to another will grow your business at no cost to you. Customers who believe in your philosophy and message are also far more likely to purchase your materials and sign up for your courses. Ask yourself these questions: What is the value to you in building better customers? How can you accomplish this by offering online courses? How do you accomplish this in the type of marketing you undertake and the type of people you attract with your messages?

CHAPTER 6

CREATE DISTINCT DIFFERENTIATION IN THE MARKETPLACE

How widespread is online education among your peers? As it turns out, it is not as widespread as you might think. Less than 1 percent of authors, experts, and thought leaders offer online courses. Less than 0.5 percent of them offer a curriculum or comprehensive online university. Sounds like an opportunity, doesn't it?

An overwhelming number of speakers are out there, competing to share their ideas with the same audience you seek to reach. What draws a meeting planner to select you over the competition? Why should the client select you over the ten other sales trainers being considered?

When a prospective client says, "What makes you different from the X other speakers/consultants on the same topic," what do you say in return? Whatever it is that you say, don't you think your competitors are saying the exact same thing?

By developing online courses, you'll dramatically differentiate yourself from the competition. You can tell the prospect proudly that you offer an array of learning products, including self-paced online learning, and these products serve as reinforcement to your in-person work while increasing knowledge retention amongst those with whom you work.

"An organization's **ability to learn** and translate that learning into action is the **ultimate competitive advantage**," says Jack Welch, former CEO of General Electric.

You make yourself more competitive when you translate your invaluable expertise into an online format.

Application Questions: Consider an admirable writer, speaker, or leader in your field. Does he or she offer an online course or university? Conduct an online search for people whose work is similar to yours. What do you like about their websites? What do you dislike? To find out more, you may even want to reach out to some of these individuals and ask them how they got started in the online world. Perhaps they can offer you mentorship tips. At Advantage, we have a global network of published authors and content specialists who can provide you with valuable advice about building your online university.

....

CHAPTER 7

MORE PRODUCTS MEAN MORE INCOME FOR YOUR BUSINESS

The most dangerous number in business is one.

That's right, one. If your business is dependent on one customer, you should be very scared. Being dependent on one book or one speech is a recipe for business disaster. Being dependent on one primary source of income (such as speaking fees or consulting fees) is downright suicidal.

I remember what happened after September 11, 2001, when once high-flying speakers, consultants, and authors were on the verge of bankruptcy. They were so dependent on giving keynote speeches, they came tumbling down when the world stopped traveling.

What are you doing to protect and safeguard your business? What are you doing to build a moat around your fortress?

Diversity leads to stability. Simply put, more products equal more income.

Online learning is your diversity. Online learning gives you more products, which you can translate into more income.

The good news is that it isn't hard.

Pretend for a minute that you are a chef at a brand-new restaurant. You've been asked to create a menu for the upcoming week. What dishes will be on your menu?

One major item to determine is how many of the dishes contain the same ingredients. If every dish has completely different ingredients that do not overlap at all, you'll spend a fortune on food supplies. However, if most of the dishes contain chicken, for example, and 50 percent of them include onions and salt, you will be able to buy the ingredients in bulk and save a ton of money.

Online learning can be similar. Why create something new when you can reuse something already created? Repackaging your materials in various forms means you have more products to offer. Provide a book; next, provide a summarized version of that book's same ideas in an action guide; next, record a reading of your book as an audio book; next, add in exercises and develop a live workshop; and, finally, film yourself conducting a workshop to sell as a DVD home-study kit. The recycling can go on and on.

The number-one reason for migrating your content to online courses is that doing so is easy. You are taking existing content and repackaging it in a format that customers are demanding. Your ideas are powerful, so why not provide them to your customers online?

Application Questions: How can you repackage what you already have? What would it take to do that? Which delivery formats would be most effective for your audience?

the

THREE

STEPS •

to CREATING *your* ONLINE LEARNING

Welcome to the [Insert Your Name Here] Online University, where you are the chancellor and president. In this section, I will teach you the three steps to creating sustainable online learning.

Be advised that, like doing anything well, creating online courses does take time and planning. The Roman

Coliseum was not built in a day; because of that, it has lasted for centuries. Your online learning has the potential to be a substantial income stream for your business, but first it needs to be set up on a strong foundation.

This section addresses the key points of developing sustainable, manageable online learning that will remove burdens from your schedule rather than adding them.

CHAPTER 8

CURRICULUM
The Strategy and Blueprint

Have you ever built a custom home? In doing so, it is unlikely you hired a general contractor and said, "Go build." If you cared at all what the end product looked like, I would suspect you first worked with an architect to construct carefully detailed blueprints that outlined the exact specifications of the home. Then, you delivered those detailed blueprints to your general contractor and proudly proclaimed, "Go build!"

Building your online learning is much the same as building your dream home. Begin with the end in mind, and then carefully make a blueprint of exactly what you want the final product to look like.

Here is my recommended approach to topics you can consider when formulating your strategy and blueprint:

VISION

What is your definition of *success*? What do you want an online course or an entire online university to help you and your business accomplish? Being able to answer these questions clearly, before you begin work, is critical.

You can start by defining your big idea. Give your usual thirty-second elevator pitch. Does this capture your big idea? Test out your vision on people who know you well and people who do not.

CONTENT

Next, help your future customers get to know you. Who are you, anyway? Why are you credible or experienced in this field? What's your background? Just as readers may be interested in reading a book by someone who has led a fascinating life, customers will be attracted to your courses if you can ably demonstrate your expertise on the topic.

What assets do you bring to the table? For what are you most well known and visible within the marketplace? What books have you written? What workshops or seminars can you deliver? In what content areas are you most well versed? In addition, what ancillary assets do you have? Perhaps you have developed some of the following materials: a proprietary formula or system; intriguing photographs, charts, or visuals that help you make powerful points when you speak; or video clips or B-roll footage that enhance your presentation.

CUSTOMERS

Let's now think about analyzing your customers. Think again about the typical customers you sketched out in Chapter 5. What is their WIIFM, What's In It For Me? What do they want? Why would they choose to learn from you over others? Think about their primary motivation, as unlocking this and serving it will allow you to build and market your courses successfully. In addition, consider the price point your customers might be willing and able to pay to take your course or enroll in your university. Given your target customers' lifestyle and technological capabilities, what might be the best packaging of your courses? Should your courses have short, snippet modules, or be framed as longer dialogues? By keeping your audience in mind, you'll develop a curriculum that meets their needs.

CONVERSION

In terms of conversion and course creation, what are the nuts and bolts of taking your physical materials, such as books, audiotapes, and speeches, and making them available online? Create a realistic plan that will give you time to partner with professionals who specialize in online learning. Add in steps for your review so you can ensure the content is presented and designed as you wish. Finally, build in time for yourself and any other instructors who will teach your material to be trained on how to facilitate the online courses.

MARKETPLACE

Who else is out there doing what you do? Are there other content leaders delivering similar material online? What are the most common delivery options for someone in your field? After developing a complete, 360-degree view of the marketplace, you must differentiate your offering.

TECHNOLOGY

Finally, brainstorm and research the types of technology that can help you create your ideal online learning. I left this topic for last in this chapter because, quite frankly, it is the least important. Your content comes first, not the technology. If you begin with technology in mind, you may sacrifice finding the best vehicle with which to express your message.

Now that we have given some thought to the overall strategy and vision of your online learning (the blueprint), let's discuss content development and course creation.

CHAPTER 9

COURSES
Content Development

Courses are the heart of your online learning.

If you've ever selected courses to take at a university, community college, or online institution, you may recall comparing the course offerings. In making such a comparison, you would have asked questions like these: What's available? Which course description looks most interesting? What's required of me as the student? How long will the course take? Now that you are developing your own course, think about what this comparison will look like to the student as you run through the following considerations:

PACKAGING

Will the course be online only? Will you offer the online course with periodic webinars or conference calls? How about offering your online course with a moderated discussion board? Alternatively, how about offering supplemental materials to go with your online course, like books, workbooks, or example materials? What technological capabilities or equipment (such as a computer, a video camera, or Internet access) will the student or customer need?

PRICING

Will the student or customer be charged by course or by subscription? Should you sell each course individually? Should you bundle courses and sell an entire curriculum? Perhaps you should make your courses available in a per-month subscription format.

LOCATION

Will the courses be recorded at a live event or in a studio? Many instructors find it difficult to present in a studio environment because they do not have a live audience from which they can derive energy. However, in a studio presentation, the production team can control all external factors, which often results in higher quality.

LEARNING VISUALS

Will your course use a digital chalkboard? What graphics or visuals will be incorporated into your material? How will the material be presented? Consider whether you will use PowerPoint, Prezi, charts, diagrams, images, audio, streaming video, or DVDs, for instance.

COURSE LENGTH

How many courses will be part of the curriculum? Will there be levels of courses, such as beginner, intermediate, and advanced? How many classes will there be per course? As a general tip, ensure that you let students know the expectations up-front, and be realistic. Remember, they may have jobs or families as well. Spending ten to twelve hours per week on a course is reasonable and recommended for working adults; less time is acceptable, too.

Addressing these questions in a thoughtful way before starting content development is key. Otherwise, you'll dive into content creation and then be forced to answer these questions after your development is underway.

....

CHAPTER 10

CLASSROOM

Your Learning Management System

Next, let's delve into the granular details of your classroom. Think carefully about the students' experience with the following questions, as well as what will be manageable for you. Remember, the more you can automate, the more time and effort you will save on your part.

PRIVATE LABEL

Will this course be presented under a private label? The benefit of private labeling is that it maintains brand consistency. A cohesive, uniform brand is beneficial. Your consumers rely on consistent branding to feel that they know who you are (or who you represent), in terms of trust, authenticity, and credibility.

TRACKING

How will you track student involvement? Will there be a dashboard for managers on the back end? Both instructors and students appreciate knowing where they stand in regards to expectations. By providing a dashboard of metrics and stats, you give everyone access to check where they are in the course and how they measure up.

COURSE MODULES

How will you divide up your classes? Studies show that students retain most effectively when material is divided into logical chunks, which the brain can digest and categorize. Think about breaking your information down into manageable, memorable, and bite-sized ideas for students. Often it is better to hone in on one core idea and delve deeply into it, providing examples and exercises, rather than overwhelming students with a broad array of ideas presented with little depth.

ASSESSMENT

How will you assess student learning? Consider having one of the following forms of measurement: a final test; a pre-test and a post-test; a video demonstration of the new abilities; an essay; a set number of discussion posts; or a qualitative evaluation from each student about the course. Remember the value of automating assessments is a way to save the instructor time.

COMMUNITY FOR STUDENTS & CUSTOMERS

Can you develop an online community around your course? Consider the value that having an online community brings to learners: they can network, help teach each other, share epiphanies, and answer questions among themselves. By setting up a Facebook group, a LinkedIn private group, a Twitter feed, a discussion board, or another online learning forum, you can encourage your students to enrich each other. Many of these relationships and conversations will continue long after your course has ended, helping to improve the caliber of the students overall.

TESTING AND CERTIFICATION

Will you offer students testing and certification programs? Certification often appeals to students because it gives them a sense of completion and accomplishment; it also gives them a definitive item they can add to a resume or portfolio. Some courses offer a printable certificate, which gives each student a sense of completion and accomplishment. Others provide the opportunity to order a certificate through the mail to frame later.

E-COMMERCE INTEGRATION

Will you offer opportunities to purchase additional items or resources through your class? Perhaps you can partner with other relevant businesses to showcase related products, literature, or tools to students, helping to enrich their application and understanding of your material. We recommend Advantage's core e-commerce system, which is powerful and easy to use. Modular from the ground up, this system supports a variety of payment gateways out of the box, from PayPal and Authorize.net to Stripe and Dwolla. You can accept payments via the method most convenient for you.

We also offer Facebook mini-stores for your Facebook fan page. We offer tons of other advanced functions, too, such as white labeling, developing affiliate links, and setting dynamic pricing, as well as the functionality to sell physical items, like textbooks or audiobook sets.

SCORM

Will your course be SCORM-compliant? SCORM (Sharable Content Object Reference Model) is simply a collection of standards for using the scores from learning objects across platforms in web-based learning. Today, many online courses use some form of SCORM-compliant software to keep track of students' scores on knowledge checks, tests, quizzes, and assessments in order to export them easily to another software.

MOBILE READY

Will your courses be compatible with mobile devices? While this is dependent on the particular audience, most of today's learners prefer to access learning content on mobile devices, such as smartphones or tablets. If your course adapts well to different-sized screens, then your learners will be able to read those screens easily. Keep in mind that certain video formats, such as flash videos, may not come across well, or at all, in certain browsers or on certain devices. Rather than trying to figure out all of the kinks in developing mobile-compatible courses yourself, consider contacting Advantage for the answers to these specific types of questions.

These are just a few of the core questions you must address in planning to build classes and courses for your online university. In the next chapter, we'll explore the first step to creating your online learning: joining the Fast Start Online Learning Program™.

CHAPTER 11

REQUEST AN INFO-PAK AND LIVE DEMO

I f it's time to take your book, keynote speeches, or other content to the next level, and reach a potentially limitless audience, you can take the first step by requesting an Info-Pak and Live Demo.

Most authors, speakers, and thought leaders have no clue how to really make money with their content. Your online learning can move you closer to your personal income goals.

Online learning is the future of information delivery and the single greatest opportunity that exists right now for authors and experts to create money out of thin air. Advantage converts books, presentations, speeches, and other content into engaging, self-paced online courses for you to sell online. We build, support, and operate online universities that generate passive revenue for top thought leaders.

Let our experts take your seminars, conferences, or even books and make them into money-generating, credibility-building online courses. Businesses are being squeezed to cut costs and increase in-office time for employees, leading to a rapid decline in on-site training and live seminars. More and more businesses are turning to online learning. Your content must be online if you want to grow your thought-leadership business and prosper in the new, emerging economy.

Ready to get your show on the road, or rather, online? Request an Info-Pak and Live Demo. You'll walk away with an understanding of what you need to build and grow your online courses. We look forward to discussing how we can help you take your message to the world through online learning!

You are one of the entrepreneurs, business leaders, and professionals who have Stories, Passion, and Knowledge to share with the world. Let us take you to the next level. Request your Info-Pak & Live Demo Today! Give us a call at 1.866.775.1696 or by visiting LogOnAndLearnBook.com.

ABOUT THE AUTHOR

 **ADAM WITTY** is the Founder and Chief Executive Officer of Advantage Media Group, an international publisher of business, self-improvement, and professional development books and online learning. Adam has worked with hundreds of entrepreneurs, business leaders, and professionals to help them share their Stories, Passion, and Knowledge with others.

Adam is an in-demand speaker and consultant on marketing and business development techniques for entrepreneurs and authors. Adam is the author of *21 Ways to Build Your Business with a Book* and co-author of *The Book Itch*. He has been featured in *The Wall Street Journal*, *Investors Business Daily*, and *Fortune* magazine, as well as on ABC and Fox. He was named to the 2011 *Inc.* magazine "30 Under 30" list of "America's Coolest Entrepreneurs." In 2012, the Chilean government selected Adam to judge the prestigious Start-up Chile! Entrepreneurship Competition.

Adam loves to hear from readers. To connect, contact him at the following address:

Adam Witty
c/o Advantage Media Group
65 Gadsden Street
Charleston, SC 29401

awitty@advantageww.com
1.866.755.1696

REGISTER
YOUR BOOK

AND ACCESS FREE RESOURCES !

It doesn't matter where you are in the world, Adam can help you share your Stories, Passion, and Knowledge with the world in the form of online learning courses.

Visit **LOGONANDLEARNBOOK.COM** to access these free resources:

 **RECEIVE** a subscription to the Author Success University™ monthly teleseminars wherein successful authors and book marketing experts reveal their tips and tricks for marketing and growing a business.

 **REGISTER** for a webinar led by Adam Witty: "How to Quickly and Easily Create Online Courses that Expand Your Brand, Cultivate Customers, and Make You Money While You Sleep."

 **COMPLETE** Advantage's Online Learning Questionnaire and receive a complimentary Discovery Call with an acquisitions editor to help you determine if your book, keynote speech, or content are worth turning into an online course.

 **REQUEST** an Info-Pak and live demonstration to discover how transforming your content into online learning can help you and your business best.

ACCESS ALL OF THE ABOVE FREE RESOURCES BY REGISTERING YOUR BOOK AT
LOGONANDLEARNBOOK.COM

www.ingramcontent.com/pod-product-compliance
Lightning Source LLC
Chambersburg PA
CBHW072044190526

45165CB00018B/1430